92
Ses

W9-BMU-086

81160

To the Reader . . .

The **Raintree/Rivilo American Indian Stories** series
features the lives of American Indian men and women
important in the history of their tribes. Our purpose is to
provide young readers with accurate accounts of the lives of
these individuals. The stories are written by scholars, including
American Indians.

Indians are as much a part of American life today as they
were one hundred years ago. Even in times past, Indians were
not all the same. Not all of them lived in tepees or wore feather
warbonnets. They were not all warriors. Some did fight against
the white man, but many befriended him.

Whether patriot or politician, athlete or artist, Arapaho or
Zuni, the story of each person in this series deserves to be told.
Whether the individuals gained distinction on the battlefield or
the playing field, in the courtroom or the classroom, they have
enriched the heritage and history of all Americans. It is hoped
that those who read their stories will realize that many different
peoples, regardless of culture or color, have played a part in
shaping the United States, in making America the great country
that it is today.

Herman J. Viola
General Editor
Author of *Exploring the West*
and other volumes on the West
and American Indians

GENERAL EDITOR

Herman J. Viola

Author of *Exploring the West* and other volumes on the West
and American Indians

MANAGING EDITOR

Robert M. Kvasnicka

Coeditor of *The Commissioners of Indian Affairs, 1824-1977*
Coeditor of *Indian-White Relations: A Persistent Paradox*

MANUSCRIPT EDITOR

Barbara J. Behm

DESIGNER

Kathleen A. Hartnett

PRODUCTION

Andrew Rupniewski
Eileen Rickey

Copyright © 1990 Pinnacle Press, Inc. doing business as Rivilo
Books

Library of Congress Number: 89-10412

1 2 3 4 5 6 7 8 9   95 94 93 92 91 90 89

Library of Congress Cataloging-in-Publication Data

Jeffery, David.
  Geronimo.
  (Raintree American Indian stories)

  Summary: A biography of the Indian warrior whose family was
killed by Mexican troops and who led raids into Mexican and
American territory.
  1. Geronimo, Apache Chief, 1829-1909—Juvenile literature.
2. Apache Indians—Biography—Juvenile literature.   3. Indians of
North America—Southwest, New—Biography. [1. Geronimo,
Apache Chief, 1829-1909.   2. Apache Indians—Biography.
3. Indians of North America—Southwest, New—Biography]
I. Title. II. Series.
E99.A6G3244   1989   979'.00497202   [B]   [92]   89-10412
ISBN 0-8172-3404-7 (lib. bdg.)

AMERICAN INDIAN STORIES

GERONIMO

Text by David Jeffery
Illustrations by Tom Redman

Raintree Publishers
Milwaukee

The boy, whose birth name was *Goyahkla,* lived in the mountains at the headwaters of the Gila River, near the borders of what are now the states of Arizona and New Mexico. But about 160 years ago, no borders crossed the land of the Be-don-ko-he Apache Indians. In that land without borders, Goyahkla loved to hear the stories about the time before time began. This was one of the stories he heard:

There was a war between the birds, who wanted light in the world, and the beasts, who wanted darkness. Because the birds won, mankind could live. But a terrible dragon survived.

A boy, son of the rainstorm, was the last child, because the dragon had eaten all his brothers and sisters. The boy was on the mountain with his uncle, learning how to hunt deer, when the dragon appeared. It roared and said, "Boy, you are nice and fat. When I have eaten this deer meat, I shall eat you." But the boy shouted "No!" to the beast. The dragon thought the boy was foolish but brave and agreed to fight him.

For a bow, the dragon had a pine tree, and his arrows were as big as saplings. Each time the dragon shot an arrow, the boy shouted and jumped up onto a rainbow. The boy's shouts splintered the dragon's arrows, and the splinters flew under the rainbow.

Then the boy shot small arrows from his bow four times. The last shot hit the dragon's heart, and the beast fell down the mountainside.

The boy's name was *Apache.*

Goyahkla—who would be called Geronimo—listened to these old stories. From his father, he learned the tales of war and Apache history, how to care for horses, how to hunt, and how to make tools and weapons.

From his mother, he learned to pray to Usen, the giver of life. Goyahkla played hide-and-seek and raid-the-enemy with his cousins. He worked in the fields, hoeing and cultivating corn, melons, beans, and pumpkins.

"We had never seen a missionary or a priest. We had never seen a white man. Thus quietly lived the Be-don-ko-he Apache," Geronimo remembered.

7

At age seventeen, after trial and ceremony, the boy became a
man and was admitted to the council of warriors. Yet it was still
a time of peace, and Goyahkla's thoughts turned to the slender
young woman called Alope. He brought a herd of ponies to her
father as a bride price, and the young Apache Indians were
married.

"I made for us a new home of buffalo hides. Alope had made many little decorations of beads. She also drew many pictures on the walls of our home." Within a few years, three children were born to the young couple.

They, like the Apache in other bands, heard rumors of war between the Mexicans and another people, the Americans, but that was a war far distant beyond their mountains.

9

In 1850, Goyahkla (then about twenty-five years old) and his mother and Alope and the three children, plus all the Be-don-ko-he, as well as Apache Indians from other bands went south into Mexico to trade. They camped outside a town they called Kas-ki-yeh.

They traded in peace, but one day when the men returned to camp, they found that Mexican troops had killed all the warriors who were guarding the camp. All the supplies, weapons, and ponies were gone. Goyahkla found his mother—killed. His wife, Alope—killed. His three children—killed.

Nothing could be done, so the eighty Apache warriors who were still alive retreated silently north out of Mexico and back to their village. Goyahkla entered his home and saw "the decorations that Alope had made—and there were the playthings of our little ones. I burned them all, even our tepee."

One day Goyahkla went out of the village alone and heard a
voice call his name four times. The voice said, "No gun can ever
kill you. I will take the bullets from the guns of the Mexicans . . .
and I will guide your arrows." Goyahkla had been given a
special "power," like a boy who could leap onto rainbows. He
went to the great Apache chiefs—Cochise, Mangas-Coloradas,
and Juh. The chiefs agreed to help get revenge against the
Mexicans.

The chiefs made all the families of their villages hide in secret places. The Apache warriors, painted for war and wearing war bands tied around their foreheads, set off in three divisions for Mexico. Taking three days' rations, and killing game for food as they went, the Apache warriors walked along rivers and over mountains. They traveled fourteen hours a day, day after day, until they came to the town of Arizpe.

Two companies of Mexican horse soldiers and two companies of Mexican foot soldiers came out to fight. The Mexicans advanced and fired. Most of the Apache warriors charged, but some went around behind the Mexicans. One Apache fought harder than any other. He was Goyahkla, who was named the leader of the battle by the Apache chiefs. The Mexicans called him "Geronimo." The name, *Goyahkla,* no longer existed. The warrior was now and forever—*Geronimo.*

Geronimo said, "In all the battle I thought of my murdered mother, wife, and babies—of my father's grave and my vow of vengeance, and I fought with fury. Many fell by my hand. . . . Over the bloody field, covered with the bodies of Mexicans, rang the fierce Apache war whoop."

Most of the Apache were satisfied with the victory, but Geronimo wanted more revenge. He led another raid into Mexico with only two other men, who were killed. Geronimo was surrounded but escaped after killing two Mexicans with arrows.

Geronimo was blamed for losing his men. However, he planned more raids because, he said, "My feelings toward the Mexicans did not change—I still hated them and longed for revenge."

15

About this time, some Americans began to move through Apache territory. They were surveying a new border between the United States and Mexico after the war between those two countries was over.

Geronimo and other Apache leaders let the Americans pass through in peace, but there was one big problem. As part of the peace with Mexico, the Americans had promised to keep the Apache from raiding Mexican territory.

That did not stop Geronimo. He and his warriors often crossed into Mexico. Sometimes they brought back mules or horses or cattle. Sometimes the Mexicans drove them off and even followed them into Arizona. Some of the Apache warriors were killed, but more of the Mexicans died in the fights.

The Apache Indians began to have trouble with American miners coming into their country looking for gold and copper. Other Americans came to make treaties for Indian land. One treaty allowed the Apache to keep the best places for gold, silver, and copper, but that agreement was rejected by the United States Senate.

Still, it was mostly a time of peace. In 1859, the Apache helped an American drive 1,200 head of cattle across their territory to the high plains of Texas. Chief Cochise even protected coaches and travelers passing through on the California Trail.

But the miners had found gold and started to make worse trouble for the Apache—even bringing in Mexicans as workers. Chief Mangas-Coloradas wanted to make peace with the miners. Geronimo and others told him to stay away from the miners—that they couldn't be trusted. Geronimo was right. When Mangas-Coloradas rode into the miners' camp, they jumped him, tied him to a tree, and lashed him with bullwhips.

When he escaped, Mangas-Coloradas went on the warpath, and Cochise and Geronimo went with him. They struck hard, taking the corn and sheep of the Mexican workers and the miners' horses. They attacked settlements and a wagon train heading for California, killing 16 men and taking 400 cattle and 900 sheep.

The Indians, including Geronimo with his new wife and family, observed American soldiers pulling out of their territory in 1861. The Apache thought they had won, but the troops were leaving to fight in the American Civil War.

In a year the soldiers were back, and again Mangas-Coloradas was tricked. He and his people were promised good treatment and supplies if they would go to a place called Apache Tejo. They went under a flag of truce, but the chief was taken prisoner. This time Mangas-Coloradas was not whipped. He was shot to death. To Geronimo this was the "greatest of wrongs" done to the Apache tribe.

Geronimo and his band were attacked time after time. Once American troops surprised his camp. He said that the soldiers "killed seven children, five women, and four warriors; captured all our supplies, blankets, horses, and clothing; and destroyed our tepees. We had nothing left. Winter was beginning, and it was the coldest winter I ever knew."

His people survived by going to live with another Apache band under Chief Victorio, a kindness that Geronimo never forgot.

In 1871, the United States government decided to settle all the Apache bands on reservations and sent General George Crook, a famous Indian fighter, to enforce the rules. After some problems, there came a time of peace. It seemed as if the Apache would be left alone and allowed to live where and how they wished.

Then—to save money it was said—the government decided to force all the different groups of Apache from their homelands and to move them to the San Carlos Reservation in Arizona. In 1876, Geronimo said that he would come with his people. Yet, in the end, he could not bear to go to that hot, dry, and barren place, so he and some others escaped.

The Indian agent, John Clum, got very angry at Geronimo and began to blame him for everything that went wrong. He said, "If only Geronimo had been hanged." Clum tricked him into a meeting. Geronimo was surrounded, put in chains, and taken to San Carlos where he was kept prisoner for four months. After he was released, Geronimo stayed near San Carlos for two years. When more and more soldiers kept riding into the region, he became worried.

"We thought it more manly to die on the warpath than to be killed in prison," Geronimo recalled. He escaped into the mountains with Chief Juh and 250 Apache. They went south to Mexico where they stayed for about a year, raiding and fighting Mexican troops.

81060

Meanwhile, General Crook had been sent back to Arizona. He saw that the reservation Apache were too crowded at San Carlos and let them move out. Then, with the help of Apache scouts he hired, the general prepared to find Geronimo and others in Mexico.

After searching through the Sierra Madre mountains, the general went out alone to meet Geronimo. They talked about exchanging prisoners, and Geronimo told General Crook of the wrongs done to his people. They made a truce, and the Apache people celebrated. Geronimo was suspicious, but he and the other renegade leaders agreed to return to the reservation.

The Apache made their way back to the reservation slowly, each band in its own time, and settled on better land with the help of Lieutenant Britton Davis. General Crook could then report that "every member of the Apache tribe is at peace."

Soon, however, a small dispute got out of control. Geronimo, Naiche (the son of Cochise), and other leaders rode off the reservation, capturing guns, supplies, and animals as they went. Again they went to Mexico, and again the American soldiers followed them.

After riding and hiding and fighting, Geronimo once more agreed to meet with General Crook. On March 25, 1886, Geronimo told the general of all the bad things done to him, to his band, and to all the Apache.

He said, "The Earth-Mother is listening to me, and I hope that all may be so arranged that from now on there shall be no more trouble and that we shall always have peace."

General Crook did not believe Geronimo's tales of bad things done to the Apache, and he demanded unconditional surrender.

Geronimo was the last of the Apache leaders to submit, saying, "Once I moved about like the wind. Now I surrender to you, and that is all."

But he did not surrender for long. He, Naiche, and others once again escaped. The army sent a new officer, General Nelson Miles, to search for Geronimo and the renegades. The general ordered five thousand troops to bring in less than two dozen Apache warriors, but the soldiers couldn't catch a single one. The Apache circled back into United States territory, raiding and also killing. As Naiche said, "We had to if we wanted to live."

The renegades went again to Mexico, but a small detachment under Lieutenant Charles B. Gatewood found them. He told Geronimo that General Miles had ordered Geronimo to surrender and be sent to Florida "or fight it out to the bitter end."

The other Apache decided to surrender, and Geronimo said to his comrades, "You have been great fighters in battle. If you are going to surrender, there is no use my going without you. I will give up with you." It was the end of his fighting. There were no more rainbows to leap upon. The dragons had won.

Geronimo and his people were sent to Florida. Geronimo was later sent to Alabama and finally to Fort Sill, Oklahoma. By then, he was an old man but still a prisoner of war.

Geronimo was allowed to go under escort to the 1904 world's fair in St. Louis. He sold his autograph and photographs of himself and saw many strange things—fighting Turks, a woman who recovered when cut in half, trained white bears, a Ferris wheel, and much more.

In 1905 at the request of President Theodore Roosevelt, Geronimo went to Washington, D.C., and rode in the inaugural parade for the new president. The crowds shouted, "Hurrah for Geronimo!" He met with the president the next day and pleaded that he and his people be sent back to Arizona. But President Roosevelt feared more bloodshed and did not give his permission.

Four years later, Geronimo died without realizing his last hopes of seeing his beloved mountains. But his name has lived on. During World War II, American soldiers who parachuted out of airplanes to attack the enemy yelled *Geronimo!* as they leaped into the sky. They, too, were fighting for freedom.

HISTORY OF GERONIMO

1829	Goyahkla (Geronimo) was born. The first volume of the *Encyclopedia Americana* was published in Philadelphia, Pennsylvania.
1850	While Goyahkla (Geronimo) and his people were in Mexico to trade, some Mexicans murdered his family.
1859	During a time of peace, the Apache Indians helped an American cattleman drive 1,200 head of cattle across Indian territory.
1861	When the American soldiers left Apache territory to fight in the Civil War, the Apache warriors thought they had driven them out of the country.
1886	Geronimo surrendered to General Nelson Miles. The Statue of Liberty was unveiled and dedicated by President Grover Cleveland.
1894	Geronimo is moved to Fort Sill, Oklahoma, where he remained until his death.
1904	Geronimo appeared at the world's fair in St. Louis to sign autographs and photographs.
1905	Geronimo rode in Theodore Roosevelt's inaugural parade.
1909	Geronimo died. The Lincoln penny replaced the Indian-head penny.